TEA AT REID'S

Illustrated by Manfred Markowski

THE STORY GOES THAT ...

*in 1346, Robert à Machin and his love Anne d'Arfet (from a wealthy
family that strongly opposed the match) fled from Bristol on a small
ship and sailed towards France. A violent storm carried them off
course until they managed to land on Madeira. Sadly Anne soon
died, followed by Robert a few days later, reportedly of the proverbial
broken heart. The story of the lovers and the discovery of the island
was carried by survivors from the ship's crew, who managed to build
a raft and sail away from the island. Word of their find eventually
reached Lisbon, and the Portuguese, the most far-ranging sailors of the
time, began searching for the island. The little town of Machico bears
Machin's name.*

'*TEA – AFTER TENNIS ON THE BALCONY.*'

This photograph is taken from the personal album of a guest. Decades later, the album was donated to the collection of Reid's Palace Hotel.

I had Tea at Reid's

The travelling connoisseur's world is full of places synonymous with certain rituals. You have Sacher Torte in Vienna, you have a Singapore Sling at Raffles, you must have been to the lobby of The Peninsula, the Oak Room at The Plaza, and a visit to the Great Pyramid is basically meaningless if you haven't stayed at Mena House.

And, of course, there's Tea at Reid's. This legendary hotel on the island of Madeira, in the Atlantic Ocean, on the edge of Europe, has its name engraved on the holy tableau of The Most Famous Hotels in the World. 'I had tea at Reid's' is written on almost every postcard sent from Madeira by distinguished globetrotters. For many it is the fulfilment of a long-nurtured wish, for some it is linked to personal memories of all sorts and natures.

This little book is your companion to Tea at Reid's. By the way, I trust you just had Afternoon Tea. I know how you feel. You have had a lot to eat.

Now you can lean back in your comfortable chair on the verandah. Enjoy the mild breeze of the early evening. There is nothing else to do but observe the busy waiters removing your trays, which you've emptied bit by bit – or should we say bite by bite?

Have you ordered the queen of all wines, a glass of champagne, to celebrate the occasion? The waiters serve it in elegant flutes. The sparkling wine sends its little bubbles up towards heaven. Above you, the seagulls circle majestically. Don't they lead a wonderful existence? Carefree, floating, seemingly weightless in the evening sky. At Reid's they say that the seagulls float on the champagne bubbles.

Such are our thoughts. Cheers! As you enjoy your champagne, the sun sends its last fire-red rays over the roof into the Bay of Funchal.

What a day – you had Tea at Reid's.

Andreas Augustin

SMALL TALK A LA REID'S

Amy Johnson (white dress) enjoys a chat with HRH Princess Marie Louise of Hanover and Cumberland while having tea on the terrace of Reid's Hotel. Amy was the first woman in history to fly from England to Australia: "So far my longest flight had been 140 miles to my home in Hull and I had never even crossed the Channel. I was rather surprised at my own audacity." (more on page 55)

A BRIEF HISTORY OF TEA

The world consumption of tea almost equals that of all other manufactured drinks put together. Today tea may be sold at auctions in producing countries such as Mombasa in Kenya, Colombo in Sri Lanka and Limbe in Malawi. Both north and south India have auction centres. Indonesia sells tea in Jakarta. China sells her tea by numbered standards at commodity fairs in Guangzhou. Tea prices are governed by quality, supply and demand. Tea brokers act as intermediaries and taste, value and bid on their clients' behalf.

Tea may also be sold from tea gardens by private sale or at offshore auctions whilst on route to its destination, for example at (new) tea trading spots in the Middle East.

Tea pickers in Sri Lanka. Tea plantations offer work for a great number of people. Female labour was and still is exploited. In 1876, the disastrous effect of the coffee-leaf disease led the planters of Ceylon to concentrate on tea.

In 2737 BC, according to Chinese legend, the virtues of tea (pronounced té in Amoy dialect) were discovered by the mythical emperor Shen Nung, to whom most agricultural and medicinal knowledge is traced. One day, legend has it, Shen Nung was sitting beneath a tree while his servant boiled drinking water, when some leaves from the tree blew into the water. Shen Nung decided to try the drink. The tree was a Camellia sinensis. Today we call this drink tea.

879: The earliest record of tea in an occidental context is said to be found in the statement of an Arabian traveller, describing the main sources of revenue in Canton as duties on salt and tea.

1210: From China the knowledge of tea was carried into Japan. Tea cultivation also spread into Tonkin and Cochin China.

1285: Marco Polo recorded the deposition of a Chinese minister of finance in 1285 for his arbitrary augmentation of the tea taxes.

1557: Portugal established a trading port in Macau and word of the Chinese drink spread quickly. Portuguese ships carried tea back to Europe. The first records of tea drinking on Madeira date from this period. The Portuguese are the only people in the Western world who call tea 'chá', from the Chinese 'chai'.

1559–1610: Travellers like Giovanni Batista Ramusio, L. Almeida and Taxiera mentioned tea.

1600: Portugal controlled most European trade with India and the Far East (an area known then as the Indies).

Queen Elizabeth I gave a royal charter to a new trading company, the British East India Company, which had a monopoly over all British trade with the Indies.

1610: A Dutch East India Company ship brought the first green tea leaves to Amsterdam from China.

1618: Tea was first offered by China as a gift to Czar Michael I, but the Russian ambassador who tried the drink did not care for it and rejected the offer. From 1689, tea was regularly imported from China to Russia via a caravan of hundreds of camels travelling the year-long journey, making it a precious commodity at the time.

Madame de Sévigné remembered Mr. Landgrave drinking 40 cups every morning.

1630s: Tea enjoyed a brief period of popularity in Paris. Around that time Madame de Sévigné, who chronicled the actions of the Sun King in a famous series of letters, noted: 'Considering the Princess of Taranto ... who takes 12 cups of tea every day ... which, she said, heals all its evils. She assured me that Mr. Landgrave was drinking 40 cups every morning. He was dying, and the tea brought him back to life before our eyes.' A certain Marquise de la Sablière launched the custom of adding milk to tea. 'Madame de la Sablière took her tea with milk, as she told me the other day, because it is to her liking,' (Madame de Sévigné).

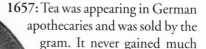

1657: Tea was appearing in German apothecaries and was sold by the gram. It never gained much esteem except in coastal areas such as *Ostfriesland*. Liselotte von der Pfalz said it tasted like boiled hay. Lessing couldn't live without it. Goethe loved tea.

1662: England's King Charles II (1630-1685) in exile married the Portuguese princess Catherine of Braganza (1638-1705).

Catherine of Braganza (1638-1705).

Just for the record: as part of her dowry this Portuguese princess brought tea to England.

By the way: Catherine's dowry was the largest ever recorded in world history.

Catherine's dowry was the largest ever recorded in world history. Portugal gave to England two million gold crusados, Tangiers and Morocco in North Africa, Bombay in India, and the permission for the British to use all the ports of Portuguese colonies in Africa, Asia and the Americas, giving England her first direct trading rights of tea.

Charles and his wife Catherine – returning from exile in the Netherlands with Dutch Delftware, as 'china' porcelain was still too expensive to be produced in Europe – were confirmed tea drinkers. When the monarchy was restored, legend has it that Catherine had a chest of tea as part of her dowry. Upon arrival in England, she asked for tea – but all she got was a glass of ale. Tea was quickly introduced at court as the drink of choice in English society, replacing beer as the national drink.

Venus her Myrtle, Phoebus has his bays;
Tea both excels, which she vouchsafes to praise.
The best of Queens, the best of herbs, we owe
To that bold nation which the way did show
To the fair region where the sun doth rise,
Whose rich productions we so justly prize.
The Muse's friend, tea does our fancy aid,
Regress those vapours which the head invade,
And keep the palace of the soul serene,
Fit on her birthday to salute the Queen.

1663: Poet and politician Edmund Waller made tea fashionable by presenting a poem to Catherine in honour of the Queen's birthday.

This subtle promotion of tea prompted the upper class to try it. Tea – the muse's friend! That was an offer too tempting to resist! The British East India Company started importing Chinese tea to England.

For a long time they also brought delicate porcelain from China to serve tea in style. At home, a whole collection of new cutlery was invented.

1660–1689: Tea sold in coffee houses was taxed in liquid form. The whole of the day's tea would be brewed in the morning, taxed by a visiting excise officer, and then kept in barrels and reheated as necessary throughout the rest of the day. A visitor to the coffee house in the late afternoon would be drinking tea that had been made hours before in the early morning. It could also very well happen that there was no more tea at all!

A whole collection of new cutlery was invented to conquer the challenges of this new drink.

In noble households, once tea had been served, the servants would make tea for themselves from the used tea leaves, and then sell the twice-used leaves at the back door.

Mischievous tea traders from the lower classes successfully undercut prices by 'blending' tea with ash tree leaves boiled in iron sulphate and sheep's dung, calling it 'smouch'.

French teacup, Chantilly, ca 1770.

1700: Tea was served in over 500 coffee houses and tea shops in London alone. While coffee houses were generally for men only, tearooms allowed even unaccompanied female patrons.

1746: William Cooksworthy found 'China Clay' in Cornwall, and developed a way to process it into fine porcelain pieces. They were called 'china-wares', to distinguish them from ordinary earthenware. Josiah Wedgwood (1730–1795), a potter, kept his prices at an acceptable low, finally allowing all classes to enjoy tea in a decent teacup. Josiah Spode's production was good enough to render the import of Chinese porcelain insignificant.

1773: In protest against horrendous taxation, British tea, imported by the British East India Company, was boycotted in America, leading to the 'Boston Tea Party', an event that helped spark off the American Revolution.

Sandwiches at Reid's Palace Afternoon Tea. In 1762, John Montagu, the fourth Earl of Sandwich, had his hands full, literally. As First Sea Lord, he commanded the mighty British Navy, was a noted explorer, and also a dedicated gambler with a love of day long card games. This led to little time for food, so he came up with the ingenious idea (some say at the card table) of putting meat between two slices of bread to eat great food without too much fuss. Today the current 11th Earl of Sandwich's family runs a popular fast-food chain by the name of Earl of Sandwich in the US.

1784: Tea was useful to the temperance movement. It offered an alternative to alcohol. It was cheap and – made from boiled water – safe to drink. Preachers of temperance urged people to sign a pledge to give up drinking alcohol, and millions did so.

François Duc de la Rochefoucauld reported: 'Throughout the whole of England the drinking of tea is general. You have it twice a day and though the expense is considerable, the humble peasant has his tea just like the rich man.'

1809: 'Next to water, tea is the Englishman's proper element. All classes consume it, and if one is out on the London streets early in the morning, one may see in many places small tables set up under the open sky, round which coal-carters and workmen empty their cups of the delicious beverage,' (Erik Gustaf Geijer, Swedish composer and historian).

1826: The Dutch succeeded in establishing tea gardens in Java. That year, Briton John Hornimann started packing tea-leaves into sealed paper bags, producing the first tea bag in history. In 1891, the opening year of Reid's Hotel, Hornimann was the biggest tea company in the world.

The Boston Tea Party:

Over 342 casks or 90,000 lbs (45 tons) of tea worth an estimated £10,000 (approx. £1m in today's currency) are consigned to the waters of Boston harbour.

Victorian silver tea set

TIME FOR TEA

Bread and water can so easily be toast and tea.
Proverb, around 1850.

Tea – always green – was drunk at breakfast by all social classes, accompanied by bread or toast, cold meats and pies, eggs and fish. Poorer families usually began the day with a cup of tea, as well as bread and butter, or perhaps porridge or gruel. Tea was then drunk at regular intervals throughout the day.

1834: In Assam, India, a wild tea plant was discovered. The fact that a genuine tea-plant was a native of Upper Assam in India was bound to break the Chinese monopoly of growing and trading tea. A committee was formed for the introduction of tea culture into India. Chinese seeds and labour were imported into the Himalaya region where The East India Company established the cultivation of tea.

1836: One pound of Assam tea made from the indigenous plant, the first modest quantity of the Assam tea production, was sent to London.

The following years the quantity increased steadily:
1837: 5 lb, 1838: twelve small boxes, 1839: 95 boxes.

1837: 'Bring me a cup of tea and *The Times*,' was Queen Victoria's first command upon her accession to the throne. The young Queen had not been allowed to drink tea in her youth, and The Times was kept away from her to avoid that she could read negative comments about the King.

THE QUEEN ON THE MORNING OF HER ACCESSION, JUNE 20, 1837.

In his *Pickwick Papers*, Charles Dickens wrote of a long brass toasting fork, which toasted bread over an open fire.

1840: At the height of the first Opium War (or Anglo-Chinese War), the Assam Company was founded.

Queen Victoria on the morning of her accession, on 20 June 1873.

Assam, Dehra, Dun, Kumaun, Darjeeling, Cachar, Kangra, Hazaribagh, Chittagong, Tarai and the Nilgiris (Madras) were developed as the eleven major tea districts of India by private companies:

At that time, according to legend, one of Queen Victoria's (1819-1901) ladies, Anna Maria Stanhope (1783-1857), the wife of the 7th Duke of Bedford, suffered from 'a sinking feeling' about four hours in the afternoon. She invited friends to join her for a meal at five o'clock in the rooms of Belvoir castle, serving small cakes, bread and butter sandwiches, an assortment of sweets and tea. On her return to London she invited friends for 'tea and a walk in the fields.'

She triggered off an elaborate fashion. Decades later ladies withdrew themselves in the afternoon

Tea is auctioned upon arrival.

to change into loose-waisted tea gowns; soft, diaphanous, festooned with lace furbelows (see page 64).

1840s–60s: The tea clippers raced between China and England for a faster delivery of tea. Bets were placed on the arrival time of ships. Tea was by now liberated from monopoly. It was auctioned upon arrival on English soil.

1860: Queen Victoria began a tradition that Queen Elizabeth II still continues today. Tea was served in the private gardens of Buckingham Palace.

There are few hours in life more agreeable than the hour dedicated to the ceremony known as afternoon tea. (Henry James)

1869: The reign of the tea clippers was brief and glorious. The Suez Canal opened, creating a navigable passage between the Far East and the Mediterranean. Overnight, it became economically viable for steamships to ply the China tea trade. Cutty Sark, launched from the Clyde on 22 November 1869, was one of the last tea clippers to be constructed.

1873: Tea was imported duty free into the United States of America.

1876: The disastrous effect of the coffee-leaf disease led the planters of Ceylon to concentrate on tea, developing that industry in remarkable time, quickly establishing tea as the island's number one export.

Tests to establish tea plantations in the West Indies, America, Brazil, Australia and the south of Europe achieved little success, mainly due to the cost of labour-intensive picking. Hence, tea remains to the greatest extent grown in its original harvesting grounds.

A Victorian sugar bowl.

From the 1880s, tearooms and teashops became popular and fashionable, particularly among women, who went there alone finding a welcoming and respectable environment in which to meet, chat and relax.

1890: One half of the world's population was drinking tea.

Now we have reached the point in history, where on the island of Madeira – off the shores of North Africa in the Atlantic Ocean – a new hotel opened its doors. It was set to become one of the most famous hotels in the world. Let's dive into the history of this wonderful island, and into the story of William Reid, the man who became a father of tourism on Madeira.

Following pages: the first photograph of Reid's New Hotel, taken in 1891, shortly after its opening.

23

Reid's New Hotel

A brief History of Madeira and

Mr. Reid's New Hotel

Today, Madeira is an autonomous region of Portugal. Its autonomy was granted after the revolution of 25 April 1974, when almost half a century of dictatorship under Salazar on mainland Portugal drew to an end.

But before Madeira was even discovered, in the

15th century, Infante Dom Henrique, Prince Henry the Navigator, gathered the finest cartographers and navigators of Portugal. Their mission was to explore the coast of West Africa.

1419: Two young sea captains, João Gonçalves Zarco and Tristão Vaz Teixeira, were blown off course on their journey around the African coast, discovering an island that they named Porto Santo.

1420: From Porto Santo, dark clouds were visible on the southern horizon. As Zarco and Teixeira approached, a giant island rose in front of them, overgrown with woods.

Reid chose architect Somers Clarke, who in cooperation with J.T. Micklethwaite submitted this drawing. It resembled – from its first impression – the view of an alpine fortress, set against a dramatic backdrop of high mountains, with a steep cliff in the foreground.

They named it Madeira (wood in Portuguese). Travelling with Zarco and Teixeira was a man by the name of Bartolomeu Perestrello. He went on to become the governor of Porto Santo and was in fact the father-in-law of Christopher Colombus.

Prince Henry immediately organised the colonisation of the island, with the first families coming from the Algarve region of Portugal.

1836: William Reid arrived on Madeira. He was a 14-year-old cabin boy from Scotland with just £5 to his name. He soon saw an opportunity in the growing number of arriving travellers and started letting farms to sun-seeking Northern European families. In the 1850s he opened his first hotels.

1860: Empress Elisabeth of Austria visited Madeira and spent five months on the island.

1888: William Reid was ready to realise his dream – to build a luxurious hotel in an unique location. Uncertain about the hotel's name he gave it the working title *Reid's New Hotel*. In the first building phase, only the west wing and the centre part of the hotel were built. Room No. 28, today at the bottom of the main staircase, was the last room of the house.

1890: William Reid, the father, died, leaving the project to his sons.

1891: William, the son, and his brother Alfred Reid, opened the hotel. The opening brochure said: 'The house is constructed in sets of singles and suites of rooms, with separate marble balconies, at different levels, with large public entertainment and sitting rooms. ... there is splendid drinking water,

Empress Elisabeth of Austria was the first royal visitor to Reid's New Hotel.

*The **routine of hotel life** was as follows:–*

In the early morning, tea and light refreshments.

At nine o'clock, breakfast, either table d'hôte, or served in private rooms.

At eleven a.m., broth, beef tea, &c., for invalids.

Luncheon at one o'clock (table d'hôte).

Tea at half-past four, in the drawing room.

Dinner at seven p.m.

29

Phase 1: the building stretched no further than today's Salon 28.

Phase 2: the extension ignores the original plans.

Phase 3: note the lift to the landing pier and sea pool.

and the grounds contain tennis courts and a pool into which the tides flow – an especially prominent feature in our new business.' *(Hotel brochure)*

1893: Reid's emerging fame reached distant shores (see Empress Elisabeth I of Austria, page 50)

1914–1918: World War I; hotel partially closed.

1919: Slowly, tourism rediscovered Madeira. In the following years the hotel was totally refurbished.

1925: Reid family sold the hotel. During this decade Madeira and the Riviera were the chosen destinations for aristocracy and renowned artists.

1937: The hotel changed owner again and was bought by the Blandy family who had arrived in Madeira at the beginning of the 19th century.

1921: After-noon tea was served where the two big pools are today. Open air dances were among the highlights of the week.

31

1921: Madeira: dependent upon the shipping facilities afforded by the various steamship companies such as the Union Castle Mail Ship Company or the Royal Mail Steam Packet Co., adopted special measures with regards to the booking of rooms.

R.M.S. "ARUNDEL CASTLE," 19,023 TONS.   R.M.S.P. "ANDES."

Tricky: the homeward steamers called at Madeira one or two days after the arrival of the outward steamers. For this reason it was usually necessary to ask arriving visitors to Reid's Hotel to accept temporary accommodation until the departure of the following homeward bound steamer, when their rooms in the hotel would become available.

Arriving at and departing from Reid's New Hotel was an exciting event: first of all you had to jump from the gangway of the steamer into the motor launch of the hotel, then you had to disembark onto Reid's landing pier.

32

1937–1939: The Blandy family, successful traders in wine, shipping, coal, communications, newspapers etc., continued the expansion of the hotel.

Flying boat Hampshire in the bay of Funchal.

1940–1949: World War II. Refugees, in particular women and children from Gibraltar, arrived at Reid's. The hotel was partially closed.

After the war a flying boat service between Southampton in England and Funchal was introduced. The first airport opened on the neighbouring island of Porto Santo. Winston Churchill arrived.

1966: Reid's opened the east wing.

1968: Two pools were opened.

1970: Reid's joins marketing organisation *The Leading Hotels of the World.*

1974: The army seized power in Portugal ending nearly 50 years of dictatorial rule.

1986: Reid's became A Select Member of *The Most Famous Hotels in the World.*

Reid's New Hotel

Beef and veal are excellent. Our hams and bacon are imported from an English country farm. There is no season in the year in which our tables do not abound with a great variety of fresh vegetables and fruits, of many of which we are the sole growers.

Our fruits include the orange, the custard apple, mango and alligator pear, besides the guava of several kinds, the loquats, apples, pears, and walnuts, besides imported dried fruits. Gooseberries and cherries appear in spring as in England, but earlier, and in summer our markets furnish many varieties of plums, apricots, figs and peaches. Bananas are in season all the year round.

Our terms vary with the size of the rooms and extent of accommodation, but may be generally stated as from £12 upwards for a single bedroom for a period of four weeks, inclusive of table d'hôte meals and light refreshments, and the use of public rooms and general advantages.

We offer special terms for larger parties, and liberal arrangements for servants. Wines, homegrown and imported, are supplied at moderate figures, and other extras are few and insignificant. Our wine carte, besides all the varieties of Madeira wine, includes all the most famous brands of Champagne, and imported beverages.

Double rooms from ($100)	£ 22.4.6
Sitting room	6.0.0
Servant's room and meals	6.0.0

Reid's New Hotel description, 1891

1990s: At Reid's, new wings, bars and restaurants were added. The former staff quarters were converted into a casual, fine restaurant, Villa Cliff, today Villa Cipriani. The strict dress code disappeared. Nowadays, black ties are only required at Christmas and Easter, in the hotel's Dining Room.

1996: Reid's was taken over by Orient-Express Hotels and reverted to its original name Reid's Palace.

2000: The new airport of Madeira opened.

Today: Madeira is a short flight away from all major European cities. The unique atmosphere of Reid's is enjoyed by its guests more than ever before.

MANAGING REID'S HOTEL

Luigi Gandolfo since 1920	George Harngartner 1978–1989
John Paquot 1939–1952	Peter Spaeth 1989–1993
António Foerster 1952–1958	Kurt E. Schmid 1993–1997
Jean G. Burca 1958–1969	Anton P. Kueng 1997–2003
R.N. Newton, as resident manager 1969–1970	Bruno Brunner 2004–2008
René Jean 1970–1972	Sandro Fabris 2008–2010
Henry Soldati 1972–1978	Ulisses Marreiros 2010–

Next pages: Overlooking the Atlantic Ocean from a comfortable resting place.

THE ETIQUETTE OF TEA

One doesn't simply drink tea: one takes tea. Some of us may harbour legitimate doubts about an institution that isn't quite sure what comes first: cream or jam, tea or milk, pinkie up or down? While some of us argue that you should first add the jam, followed by the dairy (butter or cream), for many of us nothing is more logical than the complete opposite. The same thing must be said about adding milk to tea, or, respectively, tea to milk. There are social gaps. At certain parties you are best advised to put the milk in last. This hasn't answered the question as how to drink it though – or indeed whether to crook your little finger or not.

The Maître d'hôtel and his executive chef (right), posing proudly in 1922.

You see, surrounded by these pressing issues we should simply agree to establish a basic etiquette of taking tea.

Sometimes a royal visitor graces the terrace at tea-time. Sometimes you see a queen from the distance. Here it's Cunard's Queen Elizabeth 2 'QE2' on her last visit to Madeira in 2008.

Nelson and part of his devoted team.

High - or Low Tea

This is easy: don't think of High Tea as an event for the 'High Class'. You will be surprised to hear that in this case 'high' or 'low' is simply a reference to the height of seating. In fact, low tea stands for lower tables in the sitting room, sofas and fauteuils and sufficient time to spend afternoons drinking tea rather than at work (attributed to the upper class).

High tea – yes, you guessed it right – is served on high tables. You formally sit down to a meal, while tables are laid with cutlery. The dishes bear exotic names, making up for less exciting ingredients, such as *Welsh rarebit*, white bread soaked in red wine, topped with Cheddar cheese. Or *Pan Haggarty*, a meal combining nothing more than layers of potatoes and onions.

... AND AT **REID'S**?

At Reid's the tables in the hall are low, and on the terrace they are high. To save us all the trouble of deciding if we are having *high* or *low tea*, we are confronted here with the elegant solution, served at notable establishments, called *Afternoon Tea*.

Tea pot and strainer.

HOW TO MAKE TEA:

A perfect pot of tea should be made – with certain personal preferences to be taken into account – in the following manner. Just before the water starts to boil, you warm the tea pot with a dash from the kettle, swirling the hot water around to ensure that the pot is warm enough to keep the water at the boiling point. Only then will the tea leaves open properly.

We are hesitant to suggest how much tea you should put into the pot. For many of us, the rule is one teaspoon for each person plus one for the pot (that would be strong – or as many would have it – proper tea). It all depends on the tea, how strong you like it and how its leaves open (for example Chinese Gunpowder leaves come curled and multiply their volume while brewing – even one spoon can be enough for the whole pot). Small leaves and tea dust as in tea bags keeps its size. Therefore, please find your own measurements.

The brewing time is again a matter of personal experience; three to six minutes, depending on the size of the leaves. Tea bags with low quality tea dust can give you a result within a minute.

Boiling water is for many inseparable linked to the whistle of a kettle. Of course today we boil our water in stylish Russell Hobbs accessories, a Siemens Porsche kettle with automatic switch off or any other high performance boilers.

But the good old classic kettle, like the porcelain - enameled Le Creuset steel tea kettle, for example, with a whistle alerting you when the water has begun to boil, still has a nostalgic touch.

41

We do encourage the idea of separating the freshly brewed tea immediately from the tea leaves once the tea has reached the desired strength (otherwise you talk about the 'wasted pot', where tea leaves continue to stew, producing tannin). Pour it into a second (warm) pot using a strainer.

Green tea could be brewed twice (but the second brew is different in taste and effect), black tea not. An acceptable solution are tea-balls, various infusers and t-sacs, made from unbleached, chlorine-free paper (disposable bags which you fill with your preferred tea).

How to take Tea?

After you have chosen your blend of tea, or – if you wish – coffee, the Afternoon Tea ceremony starts. All courses are served according to protocol.

With the arrival of the tea and hot water pots, you have to start calculating the strength of your tea and make decisions as to how to handle it (see above). Pour the tea first, add sugar (if at all), then add milk or lemon. Please use a fork to add lemon to your tea. Then the sandwiches arrive. English family tradition had it that they should all be eaten, before you are allowed to touch the sweets.

The Milk Question:

Hot fresh boiled tea is so hot that any non-porcelain cup could crack. As porcelain was always more expensive than pottery, to pour tea first and add milk later is considered a sign of being able to afford expensive porcelain.

Don't be confused by the name 'cream tea', which refers to the clotted cream served with the scones. The tea is still served with milk, even if it's a 'cream tea'.

You usually don't add sugar or milk to green teas.

WHAT TO AVOID, WHAT TO DO ...

Do not stir your tea. In general, avoid any noisy contact between silverware and porcelain. Instead, gently move the teaspoon from the six o'clock position toward the 12 o'clock position and back. Don't sip tea or coffee from your spoon.

Never dunk biscuits (cookies) in your tea. Sandwiches are served and eaten first. In the West, we swallow the food before we sip the tea.

Cream, butter and preserves.

> *This is the opposite of how the Japanese tea ceremony works. In a* matcha *ceremony you chew your* wagashi, *or sweet, and sip bitter* matcha *at once for a union of flavours.*

Avoid mixing milk and lemon together, or the milk may curdle.

To raise the cup, you hold the handle with your fingertips. Try to avoid putting your fingers through the handle.

Pinkie* stays put! It is neither necessary for it to support the relatively light cup, nor a sign of style to have the pinkie stand up like an antenna screening the ether for BBC World Service. Why don't we just keep it naturally aligned with all the other fingers?

SCONES

These are cut in half horizontally. Cream is spread upon the fresh cut surface, and jam on top. If you feel adventurous, you can apply the jam first and layer cream on top. Even the experts have no opinion on this one.

* *also* pinky, *noun* informal, *the little finger. Originates in the early 19th cent.: partly from Dutch* pink 'the little finger'.

FORK, KNIFE, SPOON AND PLATES:

Even if a knife and fork have been provided, it is still acceptable to use your fingers for most tea foods. You may change your mind if faced with creamy chocolate cakes, however. When you've finished eating, place the knife and fork parallel together on your plate. Somewhere between the 4 and 6 o'clock positions will do it. The tea- or coffee-spoon goes back to where you found it, next to cup on the saucer. Meanwhile, never push away a plate that's been placed in front of you, after you've finished eating. To signal a desire to have it removed, place your cutlery on the plate as per the instructions above. The waiter will now wait until everybody at the table has completed the meal. Don't ask him to remove your plate while others are still eating. It could be awkward for him.

CAKES AND SWEETS:

They are eaten with the fork only. Cutting a cake with your knife could be interpreted as an insult to the pastry-chef. Don't worry, though. He's not often around.

NAPKINS:

Never put your napkin on the table! When you have finished, or when you must excuse yourself from the table momentarily, fold it once and hang it over the arm of your chair. The gesture of putting it on the table is reserved for the hostess. This signals the end of the tea (or of any other meal, incidentally).

Behind these magic letters R E I D'S lies the most famous tea terrace overlooking the Atlantic Ocean.

BIRDS OF PASSAGE

From the Private Album

Tourism can be defined as an intentional journey to a destination for pleasure. On that note, Madeira was for many years a landing place not for tourists but for birds of passage, a port of call on the way to South Africa, to India, to the exotic Far East.

This all changed overnight in 1869 with the opening of the Suez Canal. All that was left thereafter were the occasional South America liner and ships bound for the Cape. On one of them Winston Churchill stopped at Madeira in 1899 on his way to cover the Boer War. 50 years later, he returned as a tourist to stay at Reid's. Captain Scott called *en route* to the Antarctic. The Prince of Wales stopped off while travelling to the Cape.

During the first years of Reid's New Hotel, on 24 December 1893, 21 salute shots were fired to welcome the arrival of a true tourist, Empress Elisabeth of Austria, came to relax. Following her sojourn, Reid's developed into a secluded hideaway, much-loved by some of the most notable personalities in history.

Sisi', Elisabeth of Austria, sitting on the terrace of her suite at Reid's New Hotel, having tea, accompanied by her favourite violet-flavoured ice cream. Her eyes gaze at the seagulls passing by. Seagulls were in fact Elisabeth's heraldic animal.

EMPRESS ELISABETH, nicknamed Sisi, stayed on Madeira for the first time in 1860/61. She paid a second visit over 30 years later, on 24 December 1893 to be precise. On that occasion, she headed directly for Mr Reid's new hotel on the cliff, overlooking Funchal.

She wrote long letters to her husband, praising the quality of the hotel and the natural beauties of Madeira. She stayed until 5 February 1894.

Following the Austrian empress, Reid's became known as a harbour of seclusion for some of history's great characters. Whoever touched Madeiran soil made a point of either stay at Reid's Palace Hotel – or at the very least of taking Afternoon Tea on its terrace.

50

Let us browse through an excerpt of the list of personalities taken from The Most Famous Hotels in the World's book about Reid's Palace.

PRINCE ARTHUR OF CONNAUGHT, a grandson of Queen Victoria, patronised Reid's Hotel in 1920 on his way to South Africa, along with his wife, Princess Alexandra, Duchess of Fife. Prince Arthur was on his way to South Africa, where he succeeded Viscount Buxton as governor-general.

The Prince of Connaught arrived in 1920.

CHARLES I of Habsburg-Lothringen, the last Emperor of Austria, spent the last months of his life on Madeira, where he was exiled along with his wife Zita.

They arrived on 19 November 1921. At the beginning of his exile, Charles and his entourage stayed at Villa Victoria, an annex of Reid's Palace Hotel The expenses at Reid's noble annex soon escalated into a sum beyond the budget of Charles, who had no access to his accounts. The imperial family had no choice but to leave the expensive Reid's annex. They accepted an invitation from the family of a banker to stay at their villa, near Monte. Here Charles died on 1 April 1922. Empress Zita continued visiting her husband's grave until she died, always staying at Reid's. Just recently, Charles' son Otto signed the guest book, not for the first time.

Left: Charles I

51

We could go on for ever. Across the pages of the hotel's golden Book, we find **Sir Austen Chamberlain** or adventurers like **Carlos Viegas Gago Coutinho**, the first man who flew the South route across the Atlantic to Rio; **Captain Robert Falcon Scott**, the explorer, **Princess Hermina de Hanan**, the **Duchess d'Aosta**; **Axel, Prince of Denmark**, **HRH Edward VIII**, **Princess Marie Louise**, **HRH Prince George**, **King Umberto of Italy**, various **Dukes of Edinburgh**, the **King and Queen of Sweden**, more **Windsors**, and **Liechtensteins**, and more **Habsburgs**, of course.

The autographs of Edward, the Prince of Wales, and Axel, Prince of Denmark.

Then come presidents, ministers and guests of honour: **John Galsworthy**, long before he won his Noble Prize; novelist **John Dos Passos**, actors like **Lillie Langtry** and **Heather Thatcher**, who posed for The Sketch at Reid's pool.

There were also sporting heroes such as Olympic games tennis champion **O.G.N. Turnbull**, **Sir Malcolm Campbell**, who broke the world record for speed in a car and in the air. Party animals like **Stephen James Napier Tennant**, who spent most of his life in bed, did not miss out on Reid's.

Richard D'Oyly Carte, the man behind the operatic duo Gilbert & Sullivan (today we would call him 'the producer'), who had opened The Savoy Hotel in London with a general manager called

The view many Reid's guests enjoy most facing the gardens, overlooking the cliff right out onto the Atlantic Ocean.

César Ritz; **Edward Stone**, the architect of the Picadilly Theatre in London, and many others.

Another famous guest was the great **George Bernard Shaw**, to date the only person to have been awarded both the Nobel Prize for Literature (in 1925) and an Oscar (in 1938 for his work on the film Pygmalion). The poet arrived a year before the Nobel Prize, in 1924, to work, sunbathe and 'master the tango.' Shaw, an Irishman, left resident dancing instructor Max Rinder a photograph, inscribed with the words: 'The only man who ever taught me anything.'

Rinder with Shaw: 'The only man who ever taught me anything'.

Birkenhead stayed at Reid's frequently.

One evening, strolling into dinner at Reid's, the **Earl of Birkenhead**, former Secretary of State for India and Lord Chancellor between 1919-22, examined the photograph. Known, for his staunch opposition, the Earl curled his lip at the Irish redhead's boast. Drawing his pen he wrote below the Shawian autograph: 'Could Birkenhead teach you no law?'

To this he added: 'Do let us have a little less of your perfection, My Dear G. B. S.'

Like an eagle's view: the terrace of room 940 on top of the tower in the historic wing. The great aviator Amy Johnson, who stayed here in March 1933, certainly enjoyed it – although she took a while considering whether or not to swim in the Atlantic.

WINSTON CHURCHILL

In 1949 Reid's Hotel received a second lease of life. After being closed for nine years, it was about time for its legend to be revived. Around that time, Sir Winston Churchill – who, remember, had first stopped off at Madeira in 1899 on his way to cover the Boer War – was recovering from a minor stroke and seeking an ideal holiday destination. He found it at Reid's, staying here from 1–12 January 1950. While working on his war memoirs and painting in the nearby village of Câmara de Lobos, Churchill occupied a suite on the first floor. In honour of the great British leader, it has since been named Churchill Suite.

Winston and Clementine Churchill on the verandah of their suite: 'I have been greeted by many people in the world for whom I have done something but never in my whole life been greeted with such enthusiasm by people for whom I have never done any-thing,' noted Winston Churchill after having been received by the people of Madeira. Churchill would do for Madeira what Sisi, Empress of Austria, had done some 57 years earlier. He became the first promoter of Madeira after World War II.

57

Churchill's visit triggered off the planned renaissance of Reid's Hotel. In 1955, film director **John Huston** arrived with his star, **Gregory Peck**, to shoot **Moby Dick**. They used Reid's as base while on location on Madeira, one of the few remaining places where whalers still used open boats. Other stars of the screen like **Roger Moore** also chose Reid's.

In 1959, after his defeat by **Fidel Castro**, the Cuban dictator General **Fulgencio Batista** fled to Madeira – where he and his family spent the following two years on the second floor of the hotel.

Fulgencio Batista poses with his family at Reid's.

Empress Zita arrived every year to visit the grave of her husband. **HRH Umberto**, the last King of Italy, found a place to reflect at the hotel.

The Royal Swedish couple, King Gustav and his Queen Silvia.

HRH the King of Spain enjoyed it, too, as did **King Gustav** and **Queen Silvia of Sweden**, who stayed for three days in 1986. Meanwhile, Britain's former prime minister **Edward Heath** spent one of his last holidays here. The complete list can be found in the book REID'S PALACE.

Tea, in Quotes

Being English used to be so easy. They were one of the most easily identified peoples on earth, recognised by their language, their manners, their clothes and the fact that they drank tea by the bucketload. (Jeremy Paxman, 'The English')

Wouldn't it be dreadful to live in a country where they didn't drink tea? (Noel Coward)

Love and scandal are the best sweeteners of tea. (Henry Fielding 'Love in Several Masques')

Teaism is a cult founded on the adoration of the beautiful among the sordid facts of everyday existence. It inculcates purity and harmony, the mystery of mutual charity, the romanticism of the social order. (Okakura Kakuzo, 'Book of Tea')

Come oh come ye tea-thirsty restless ones, the kettle boils, bubbles and sings musically. (Rabindranath Tagore)

An empty teacup must immediately be refilled. (Chinese table etiquette)

I always fear that creation will expire before teatime. (Sydney Smith)

If two women should pour from the same pot, one of them will have a baby within a year. Two teaspoons accidentally placed together on a saucer, points to a wedding or a pregnancy. (Chinese tea superstitions)

Each cup of tea represents an imaginary voyage. (Catherine Douzel)

My dear, if you could give me a cup of tea to clear my muddle of a head I should better understand your affairs. (Charles Dickens)

You can never get a cup of tea large enough or a book long enough to suit me. (C.S. Lewis)

There is a great deal of poetry and fine sentiment in a chest of tea. (Ralph Waldo Emerson, 'Letters and Social Aims')

Drinking a daily cup of tea will surely starve the apothecary. (Chinese Proverb)

The perfect temperature for tea is two degrees hotter than just right. (Terri Guillemets)

There is no trouble so great or grave that cannot be much diminished by a nice cup of tea. (Bernard-Paul Heroux)

If man has no tea in him, he is incapable of understanding truth and beauty. (Japanese Proverb)

Great love affairs start with Champagne and end with tisane. (Honoré de Balzac)

Drink your tea slowly and reverently, as if it is the axis on which the world earth revolves - slowly, evenly, without rushing toward the future. (Thich Nat Hahn)

Tea's proper use is to amuse the idle, and relax the studious, and dilute the full meals of those who cannot use exercise, and will not use abstinence. (Samuel Johnson)

Remember the tea kettle - it is always up to its neck in hot water, yet it still sings! (Author Unknown)

Never trust a man who, when left alone in a room with a tea cozy, doesn't try it on.

Billy Connolly

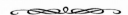

MORE ABOUT TEA

Here are a few important points for a decent dinner conversation to "tea-off" in style:

◆ Did you know that the only country in Europe where tea is cultivated is Portugal? On the islands of the Azores, tea plantations were first mentioned in around 1750. Since 1878 Chinese from Macao assisted with their know-how. The *Gorreana* tea, all made from the same plant, include Orange Pekoe, Broken Leaf, Pekoe and Hysson, a green tea.

◆ Tea is the common name of the shrub *Camellia sinensis*. The word tea came into the English language from the Chinese word for tea. The British English slang word 'char' for tea arose from its Mandarin Chinese pronunciation 'cha'.

The new Kodak model from 1904 offered a user friendly viewfinder. Visitors of Reid's – in particular ladies – produced thousands of snap shots.

◆ The four basic types of true tea are black tea, oolong tea, green tea, and white tea.

◆ There was a fashion for women to wear tea gowns. They were softer and less restrictive than evening gowns

◆ At teatime it was not always deemed necessary for women to wear gloves. Nonetheless many did, and the author of the 19th century *The Etiquette of Modern Society* points out that a thoughtful hostess should always provide biscuits with tea, since these can be eaten more easily than sandwiches without removing one's gloves.

The tea-gown became the first fashionable 'woman's at-home' dress. It appeared in the 19th century, characterised by unstructured lines and light fabrics. Erotic considerations were not the driving force behind this model.

◆ Tea's world consumption equals all other manufactured drinks (second only to water) – including coffee, chocolate, soft drinks, and alcohol – put together.

◆ In contrast to the large-scale industrial production there are many small 'gardens', sometimes minuscule plantations, that produce highly sought-after teas prized by gourmets.

These teas are both rare and expensive, and can be compared to some of the most expensive wines in this respect.

◆ Tea leaves contain more than 700 chemicals, among which the compounds closely related to human health are flavanoides, amino acids, vitamins (C, E and K), caffeine and polysaccharide. Moreover, tea drinking has recently proven to be associated with the cell-mediated immune function of the human body.

◆ *Tasseography* is a divination or fortune-telling method that interprets patterns in tea leaves, coffee grounds, or wine sediment. The terms derive from the French word *tasse* (cup).

◆ In 1904, American tea merchant Thomas Sullivan began distributing samples of his tea in small silk bags with a drawstring. Consumers noticed that they could simply leave the tea in the bag and, better still, re-use it with fresh tea. However, the potential of this distribution/packaging method would not be fully realised until later on. During World War II, tea was rationed. In 1953 (after rationing in the UK ended), Tetley launched the tea bag to the UK and it was an immediate success.

◆ Tea used in tea bags has an industry name: it is called 'fannings' or 'dust' and used to be the waste product produced from the sorting of higher quality loose leaf tea. Today tea companies also provide higher quality teas in tea bags.

◆ Tea plays an important role in improving beneficial intestinal micro flora, as well as providing immunity against intestinal disorders and in protecting cell membranes from oxidative damage. Tea's content of fluorine prevents dental caries. The role of tea is well established in normalizing blood pressure, prevention of coronary heart diseases and diabetes by reducing the blood-glucose activity.

Both green and black teas contain a number of anti-oxidants, mainly catchins that have anti-carcinogenic, anti-mutagenic and anti-tumor properties.

◆ Tea has almost no carbohydrates, fat, or protein.

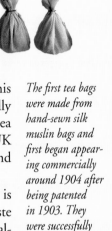

The first tea bags were made from hand-sewn silk muslin bags and first began appearing commercially around 1904 after being patented in 1903. They were successfully marketed by tea and coffee shop merchant Thomas Sullivan from New York, who shipped his tea bags around the world.

◆ Tea is a natural source of the amino acid theanine; methylxanthines such as caffeine and theobromine, and polyphenolic antioxidant catechins (often referred to as tannins).

◆ Kaempferol, a flavanoid found in green and black teas, reduces the risk of heart disease.

◆ Kombucha is a drink produced from bacteria and yeast grown on tea.

◆ ISO 3103 is a standard published by the International *Organization for Standardization* (ISO), specifying a standardised method for brewing tea. It was originally laid down in 1980 as BS 6008. It was produced by ISO Technical Committee 34 (Food products), Sub-Committee 8 (Tea).

The abstract states the following:

The method consists in extracting of soluble substances in dried tea leaf, containing in a porcelain or earthenware pot, by means of freshly boiling water, pouring of the liquor into a white porcelain or earthenware bowl, examination of the organoleptic properties of the infused leaf, and of the liquid with or without milk or both.

This standard is not meant to define the proper method for brewing tea, but rather how to document tea brewing procedure so sensory comparisons can be made. An example of such test is a taste-test to establish which blend of teas to choose for a particular brand in order to maintain a consistent tasting brewed drink from harvest to harvest.

Please note: This work was the winner of the parodic Ig Nobel Prize for Literature in 1999.

TEA IN **POP** CULTURE

'Tea for Two' was a 1925 popular song by Vincent Youmans and Irving Caesar, introduced in the musical 'No, No, Nanette'. 'Tea for Two' became a 1950 movie starring Doris Day, which reintroduced the song.

Fictional characters who prefer Earl Grey* tea include Bobby Simone of NYPD Blue, Jean-Luc Picard of Star Trek: The Next Generation, Bruce Wayne in the comic book series Batman, Dr. Eleanor Ann 'Ellie' Arroway in Contact, Frasier Crane of Frasier, Artemis Fowl of the Eoin Colfer books, Dr. Donald 'Ducky' Mallard of NCIS.

P. G. Wodehouse's Bertie Wooster preferred Darjeeling at breakfast, while Earl Grey was the preference of characters like Sir Leigh Teabing from 'The Da Vinci Code', Trent from Kim Harrison's 'Dead Witch Walking' and L and Watari from the animation movie 'Death Note'.

'Picture you upon my knee
Just tea for two
And two for tea
Just me for you
And you for me ...
alone.'

Mario Santos, from the Argentinian TV series 'Los Simuladores', always enjoyed Earl Grey tea. In the alternative history novel 'The Two Georges', by Richard Dreyfuss and Harry Turtledove, the protagonist, Colonel Thomas Bushell, had a preference for Irish Breakfast tea.

The main character from Haruki Marukami's novel 'Kafka on the Shore' frequently drinks Earl Grey. Michael Franks produced an album called 'The Art of Tea'.

*The Earl Grey blend is named after the 2nd Earl Grey, British Prime Minister in the 1830s. It is a tea flavoured with bergamot oil, taken from bergamot, a citrus fruit.

While some sunbathers still relax at the pools, the tea hour has called all the others to the terrace.

When In Rome ...

Different Countries, different Teas

Europe

A choice of different blends is standard in all restaurants, bars and tea- and coffee-houses. True afternoon teas can be found in England. Five o'clock 'teas' are often coffee, accompanied by cakes.

Irish Breakfast tea

is a full-bodied, brisk, malty brew. It is a blend of several black teas: most often Assam teas and, less often, other types of black tea. At one time there must have been a decided preference for Assam teas in Ireland. Most commonly, Irish Breakfast tea is drunk with milk, but some prefer to drink it straight or with lemon.

The Japanese tea ceremony

is literally translated as 'tea hot-water, the way of tea'. This traditional activity is strongly influenced by Zen Buddhism, in which powdered green tea, or *matcha* is ceremonially prepared and served to others.

Kashmir's Kahwah

is a celebration tea from Kashmir, flavoured with saffron and spices.

North Africa

Black or mint tea: sometimes black tea is poured from a distance to produce a foam on the tea.

Russia

has had a rich and varied tea history since 1638. Today it is considered the de facto national beverage, due in part to Russia's northern climate, closely associated with traditional Russian culture. The unique tea brewing device known as a Samovar has become a symbol of hospitality, and comfort. Traditional tea glasses are considered low class. Putting cherry jam into the tea is common.

An elegant tea stand in Penang, Malaysia.

SINGAPORE & MALAYSIA

are famous for its *Teh tarik*. The main ingredients are tea and condensed milk. Ginger water may also be added to form *teh halia*, or ginger tea.

TAIWAN

Taiwan is famous for the making of Oolong tea and green tea, as well as many western-styled teas.

THAI TEA

Thai tea *cha-yen* (or Thai iced tea) is a drink made from strongly-brewed black tea (also known as red tea in East Asia). Add star anise, tamarind or red and yellow food colouring. This tea is sweetened with sugar and condensed milk and served chilled. Evaporated or whole milk is generally poured over the tea and ice before serving – it is never mixed prior to serving – to add taste and creamy appearance. It is served in a traditional tall glass.

TIBET

Tibetan butter-tea is world-famous; the tea is first boiled for half a day, till it gets dark brown. After being skimmed, it is shaken several times in a special cylinder with some fresh yak butter and salt.

71

TURKISH TEA

Today tea is more popular than Turkish coffee among younger people. The nation's founder, Atatürk, encouraged tea as an alternative to Turkish coffee, an expensive and at times unavailable drink in the aftermath of World War I. Coffee had to be imported, tea was available locally on the eastern Black Sea coast. Turkish tea is typically prepared using two stacked kettles especially designed for tea preparation.

Tea is drunk from small glasses to show off its colour, with lumps of beetroot sugar.

U.S.A.

Most famous hotels serve afternoon tea. The column of Judith Martin, The Washington Post's 'Miss Manners', is full of good advice on the subject. America's approach to certain aspects of afternoon tea differs slightly from the original version. Some British culinary standards (such as fish-paste sandwiches, Sally Lunns, and Swiss rolls) are missing from American tea menus, however.

At the moment fashionable: 'Teddy Bear Tea', a children's party involving streamers, balloons, hearts, glitter, and all the other fancy treats children adore. That includes menus featuring peanut butter and jelly and apple cider.

When at Reid's Palace: Traditionally you are served sandwiches, before you enter the second round, with fresh scones – directly from the baker's oven – followed by pastries.

DID YOU KNOW THAT ... ?

◆ the Dining Room at Reid's was known as the House of Lords because of the number of British peers who dined there.

◆ 1960s general manager Jean Burca received a letter from a young man, imprisoned in Italy. He had robbed a bank to be able to afford a holiday at Reid's Hotel. He begged for support (he got it).

◆ during bathing hours an orchestra used to play on the upper terrace at the entrance to the lift.

◆ the hotel has both a billiards room and a bridge room. Its multi-purpose Salon No. 28 is the oldest room in the hotel. It was originally located on one corner of the very first building, which today forms the heart of the hotel.

◆ Reid's gardens display approximately 520 different types of plants on 17,400 sqm, collected and cultivated in over 100 years of devoted gardening.

The flower 'girl' of Reid's hotel, Anabela, uses approximately 12,000 flowers per year to decorate the hotel.

Advertising poster in 1928 by Madeira resident German painter Max Römer.

DID YOU KNOW THAT ... ?

◆ a wide range of lizard specimens, among them black and light coloured geckos, roam the gardens and the cliffs of Reid's Palace. They are, of course, totally harmless. Interestingly, there are no large 'wild' animals and no snakes on Madeira.

◆ the seawater pool refills automatically twice a day, whenever high tide comes in (left page).

◆ The distance between the starting point of the rope and the red buoy floating in the bay in front of Reid's sea water pool is always exactly 182 metres away from the shore.

One of Reid's regular guests: a beautifully coloured lizard.

◆ Reid's was one of the last hotels on Earth to have a diner dress code until recently. The code – black tie – is still requested during festive seasons.

The seawater pool (left) refills automatically. The red buoy (top left) is exactly 182 metres away from the shore.

A splendid Spa awaits the visitor, at the eastern end of the hotel grounds. The Spa also welcomes day visitors for treatments. All treatment rooms have a terrace and sea view.

MADEIRA - THE WINE ...

It would be wrong to leave you under the impression that tea is the only drink on the island of Madeira. There is of course this famous wine, called Madeira.

YOU SHOULD KNOW THAT ... ?

◆ regardless of the type of the grape, all Madeira wine comes from the island of Madeira.

◆ the wines are harvested during the months of September and October.

◆ grapes are mostly pressed on the spot, immediately after they have been picked.

◆ there are four types of Madeira wine: Sercial, Verdelho, Bual and Malmsey, each named after the different type of grape from which it is made.

> *Sercial and Verdelho are light and dry and can be drunk as an aperitif.*

> *Bual and Malmsey are rich, full and heavy and are traditionally thought of as dessert wines.*

◆ every French adolescent knows the words to a mildly obscene little song about the supposedly aphrodisiac powers of Madeira.

◆ Port, Sherry and Madeira are the three most popular fortified wines on the British Isles. All were developed under the influence of British wine merchants; all are fortified with the addition of brandy so that they have an alcoholic content of nearly 20%; all can be drunk as aperitifs or dessert wines; and all are relatively expensive.

79

◆ the English and French consume more of this wine than the people of any other nation (including Portugal, where it is produced), because nearly 70% of the Madeira (like Marsala wine from Sicily) is used in cooking.

◆ from 1485 Madeira wine formed part of a stipend of parish priests in England.

◆ by the middle of the 16th century it was shipped to France and the Low Countries for 3,200 reis (75p or £1) a pipe (105 gallons).

◆ in 1478 the Duke of Clarence was drowned in Madeira wine. Imprisoned in the Tower of London after plotting against his brother Edward IV, he was put on trial for treason. Following his conviction, he was "privately executed" at the Tower on 18 February 1478. The story spread that, on his own request, he was drowned in a butt of Malmsey.

A butt was equal to two hogsheads—105 imperial gallons— (477.3 litres) enough to easily drown in. A body, believed to be that of Clarence, which was later exhumed, showed no indications of beheading, the normal method of execution for those of noble birth at that time. Another possibility is that George's remains were sent to the abbey in a barrel of Malmsey, as Horatio Nelson's were sent home in a barrel of brandy.

THE MAKING OF ...

Most of the pressing is still done by human feet and, after this first pressing, the mash is further compressed by means of huge stones which are forced down by a wooden screw. The juice is then brought down to the main town of Funchal by men who carry 50 litre goatskins slung over their shoulders. Here the juice is fermented for two to four weeks before a small amount of brandy is added. The mixture is then moved to a heated room called an *estufa*, where it is gently cooked at 56 degrees Celsius for three to six months.

This heating process ages and matures the wine and takes place under strict government supervision. Special inspectors place thermostatic seals on each *estufa*, and if the temperature becomes too high the seal is automatically broken and the wine is confiscated. This is done because even though overheated wines lose much of their richness they appear older than they really are. Unscrupulous dealers might (as has been done in the past) put the wine in bottles with labels that carry prestigious dates and carry enormously high prices.

Once the heating process is over the wine rests for nearly two years. It is then blended, placed in fresh casks and fortified with additional brandy to bring it to its desired alcohol percentage. The casks are then stacked and set aside to mature for anywhere from three to five years. Once it is bottled, Madeira is a long-life wine. From time to time an 18th century bottle is found in which the wine is still quite fresh. I recently tasted a Malmsey from 1848 that was as rich, smooth and delightful as any Madeira I have ever sampled.

Sport activities have always been an important part of Reid's. However, after the consumption of Madeira wine it is not generally recommended to engage in activities such as this one.

TEA RECIPES

Take your Reid's tea experience with you! Afternoon Tea at home will no longer be the same. On the following pages you will find some recipes to help you enhance your performance on the home front.

Reid's pastry chefs prepare Afternoon Tea for a maximum of 250 guests every day. Ten chefs are in charge of the culinary elements of Reid's Afternoon Tea. Every day they bake up to 11 different types of cakes. Hundreds of scones are made just before and during tea time.

> *8,500 litres of cream flow into the sweet production per year. 200 eggs are broken on average every day. The hotel gets through seven kilograms of dark chocolate and 20 kg of melted butter per day. A British company supplies clotted cream.*

SANDWICHES

At Reid's Palace chefs prepare cheese, cucumber, prawns, salmon and avocado finger sandwiches every day. Delicate fillings are first put on long slices of bread, already sliced lengthways. Butter is spread with white flexible spatula knives for the cheese sandwiches, while the other fillings are applied directly, topped by one more slice of bread. Only then are they cut into the 'fingers'.

SPREADS

Two of the author's favourites are simple to produce: prawns and avocado.

Boiled prawns are cut in half and mixed with cocktail sauce (mayonnaise, ketchup, salt, pepper, a dash of Cognac).

For the avocado spread you mix one kg of diced avocados with 200 g diced tomatoes, season to taste. Done.

SCONES (4 scones)

Ingredients:

10 g white flour
50 g wheat flour
12.5 g butter without salt
1 tea spoon natural yoghurt
1 Egg
25 g sugar
5 g salt
37.5 g dry raisins
1.5 g baking powder

Preparation:

• Mix both flours with baking powder, sugar, salt, raisins, and butter.
• Add eggs and yoghurt and mix gently.
• Divide the dough into four and place in small paper cups.
• Let scones rest for 15 minutes and brush the tops of the scones with egg.
• Bake scones in oven, pre-heated at 180–200 °C for approximately 20–25 minutes.

Madeira cake

Ingredients:

250 g sugar
250 g unsalted butter
5 eggs
250 g flour
6.5 g baking powder
250 g candied fruit
30 g sultana grapes
0.50 cl Madeira wine

Preparation:

• Beat up the butter with the sugar very well.
• Gradually add the eggs.
• Mix the candied fruit with 250 g of flour.
• Mix the baking powder with the remaining flour and then add to the mixture.
• Add the candied fruit and finally the Madeira wine.
• Then put the cake in the oven at 170°.

Ginger cake

Ingredients:

125 g sugar

32 g unsalted butter

32 g pork fat

32 g sugar honey cane

125 g flour

125 g milk

2 eggs

4 g baking soda

6.5 g cinnamon powder

Preparation:

• Beat up the butter with sugar and then the pork fat.

• Add sugar honey cane, eggs and milk and finally the flour mixed with baking soda and cinnamon powder.

• Then put the cake in the oven at 170°.

More than memories: take a souvenir from Reid's with you.

Tea consumption at Reid's / year	Kg
❖ English Breakfast	122.0
❖ Reid's Blend	41.0
❖ China Gunpowder 'Temple of Heaven'	36.0
❖ Earl Grey	29.0
❖ Darjeeling FTGFOP 2nd Flush	24.5
❖ Ceylon Pettiagalla OP	18.0
❖ Assam TGFOP1 Hazelbank	17.0
❖ Camomile	7.5
❖ China Jasmine	6.5
❖ China Bancha	3.0
❖ Green Mate	3.0
❖ China Green Sencha	1.0
❖ Lapacho	1.0
❖ China White Snowflakes	0.5
Infusions	
❖ Fruit Garden (peach/strawberry)	6.5
❖ Black Currant	5.5
❖ Rooibos Wild Fruits	4.5
❖ Wintersweet	3.5
❖ Raspberry	3.5
❖ Bio Orange Verbena	3.0
❖ Japan Sencha	3.0
❖ Honeybush	1.8
❖ Rooibos Original	1.5
❖ Nana Mint	1.5
❖ Verbena	0.5

THE SMALL PRINT

First of all the author and his team wish to thank Sandro and Doris Fabris for the encouragement to write this little book. He is also indebted to Isabel de Portugal for her assistance in coordinating his stay at Reid's, and he is most grateful to (in alphabetical order): Luciano Bruzzone, Lisabeth Burca, Richard Burca, Paulo Coelho, Patrícia Gomes, Tânia Jesus, Anton Kueng, Nelson Martins, Rita Oliveira, Luis Pestana, Marcelino Rodrigues, Anneline Santos and Carlos Valente and all the others who helped so wonderfully to put this book together.

Valuable leads came from historical advisors like Drª Helena Araújo (Museu Vicentes, Funchal), Mag. Carola Augustin (famoushotels.org archives Vienna), João Borges (former Director of Tourism, Funchal, Madeira) and Prof. Rui Carita (Colégio dos Jesuitas, Funchal).

Advisors: Paul M. McManus (President & Chief Executive Officer: The Leading Hotels of the World), Catanho Fernandes (Diario de Notícias, Funchal).

Illustrations: Manfred Markowski

Historical Photographs: the collection of Perestrellos Photographos, Museu Vicentes, Funchal, Madeira; the Max Karkegi Collection, Vitré; Essential Madeira;, Burca Collection, Malcolm Mc Donald Collection.

Edited by Thomas Cane & Cherry Chappell

1 2 3 4 5 6 7 8 / 10 09 08
© 2008: Andreas Augustin
www.famoushotels.org
Your highly appreciated comments and suggestions
are best mailed to the
teamaster@famoushotels.org